Poetry and Reflections on Life

Greta E. Moon

Copyright © 2018 Greta E. Moon

All rights reserved. This book or any portion thereof may not be reproduced or used in any manner whatsoever without the express written permission of the publisher.

Unless otherwise noted Scripture quotations are from New King James Version (NKJV), copyright © 1982 by Thomas Nelson. Used by permission. All rights reserved

Collaboration

Editor: Shavonna Bush-All Write Editing

ISBN-13: 978-1-7323072-0-9

Turtle to Butterfly

Montgomery, AL

36116

We are God's poem spoken from His heart released in time past into the earth.

For we are His workmanship (poiema), created in Christ Jesus for good works, which God prepared beforehand that we should walk in them.

Ephesians 2:10

Table of Contents

- Mere Words
- The Life of a Seemingly Insignificant Soldier
- Meet Me Face to Face
- Substitute
- Creator's Life
- God
- The Artist
- Untitled
- A Beautiful Picture
- Not Alone
- Dreamt a Dream
- Life Changes in a Fleeting Moment
- Praise, Glory, and Honor Unto You
- Untitled
- Validation
- The Creator
- Our Gifts We Bring
- Untitled
- Untitled
- Daisy

- Untitled
- Untitled
- God, You are Awesome
- Direction
- Untitled
- Micah 4
- To the Head Cheerleader of God
- Amazing
- Untitled
- Untitled
- Heartbroken
- Untitled
- Obstacles

Thank you, God, for everyday that gives me new inspiration.

All love and praise to You my great and creative God.

For God so loved the world that He gave His only begotten Son, that whoever believes in Him should not perish, but have everlasting life.

John 3:16

And we have known and believed the love that God has for us. God is love, and he who abides in love abides in God, and God in him.

1 John 4:16

We love Him because He first loved us.

1 John 4:19

Mere Words

Mere words cannot truly express the spectrum of human emotions. Such varied emotions of love, anger, amazement seem so easily explained, but when expressed can vary greatly from relationship to relationship.

As I sit here wanting to share with You what I feel for You. No words formed from my lips could truly say what I would like for You to know. It is true when I said I love You, but that does not encompass what I feel. Everything that I have ever imagined You have placed the pieces in the puzzle. It is said that love is a many splendored thing.

Love is like the cool glass of water on the day when nothing else will quench the scorching heat. Love is like listening in the breeze for Your voice just waiting to hear it once more.

Love is sacrifice when you have nothing, but yourself to sacrifice.

Love is loving the other right where they are at in life with all the "stuff" that comes with it knowing that they will reach their potential.

Love is words that are spoken knowing the other will always listen.

In all of this it may seem that love is all of this, but love is so much more. These are mere words that cannot express real love. I could not even begin to convey what it is I feel for You. All that I can do is show you in actions of my love for You.

Isaiah 61:1; Luke 4:18; Luke 4:24

The Life of a Seemingly Insignificant Soldier

You were mocked and scorned in a country that was not Your own.

You were sent to give good news to those who were downtrodden.

You were sent to comfort and heal those hearts that had been broken by the enemy.

You have destroyed the chains of the enemy; no longer are we subject to his torture.

A life of a seemingly insignificant soldier until the very moment you were sacrificed on the battlefield.

It is then we understood that Your life has always been significant.

This is Jacob, the generation of those who seek Him, who seek Your face.

Psalm 24:6

Seek the Lord and His strength; Seek His face evermore!

Psalm 105:4

Meet Me Face to Face

Go Beyond the Call

Go Beyond the Gift

Meet Me Face to Face

Go Beyond the Here

Go Beyond the Now

Meet Me Face to Face

Go Beyond all Space

Go Beyond all Time

Meet Me Face to Face

And so I insist—and God backs me up on this—that there be no going along with the crowd, the empty-headed, mindless crowd. They've refused for so long to deal with God that they've lost touch not only with God but with reality itself. They can't think straight anymore. Feeling no pain, they let themselves go in sexual obsession, addicted to every sort of perversion.

Ephesians 4:17-19-Message Bible

Substitute

Fear has gripped me so tight

Tomorrow comes to relieve the night

Standing before a holy God I fail

Having given into flesh so frail

A future seemingly so distant

Changing my decisions in an instant

A life lived with no turning back

The battlefield of the mind is under attack

Forsaking the words you spoke so clear

Leaving the life I desired for something so near

To be intimate connects us to the inmost character off those we are in relationship with. Intimacy means we have access to the farthest reaches of their deepest desires. This type of environment of intimacy has been fastened through promotion by the individuals sense of privacy, familiarity, and comfort with one another.

Creator's Life

I am humbled by Your presence moving in me

I am pregnant with the life You brought

I am carrying within me the light of Your creativity

I am waiting for You to quicken it within me

I am willing to birth this life here upon the earth

Food for Life

John 6:35

Promise Truth

John 14:6

Always with Us

Hebrew 13:5b

Love

1 John 4:7-10

Faithful

Hebrews 10:23

Joy

1 Peter 1:8b

Blessing

Hebrews 6:13-15

Rescue

Isaiah 52:12

Drink

John 4:13-14

Forever

Revelation 1:8

God

Truth Unfailing

Never Forsaking

Love Unceasing

Filler of the Hungry

Promise Keeper

Joy Unspeakable

Immeasurable Blessing

Rescuer of All

Source of Faith

Thirst Quencher

Forever and Always

Then God said, "Let Us make man in Our image, according to Our likeness; let them have dominion over the fish of the sea, over the birds of the air, and over the cattle, over all the earth and over every creeping thing that creeps on the earth. So God created man in His own image; in the image of God He created him; male and female He created them.

Genesis 1:26-27

But when they came to Jesus and saw that He was already dead, they did not break his legs. But one of the soldiers pierced His side with a spear, and immediately blood and water came out.

John 19:33-34

The Artist

     The Artist set out at the beginning of time to paint the greatest masterpiece to have ever existed. His canvas was to be the earth. This masterpiece was never to be like any that could be painted by a human painter. At the outset it seemed so ordinary, but this painting would be strikingly different. The Artist began every brush stroke with just a word. As the words fell from His lips life sprung forth into His painting. As the ages passed over the canvas the painting would seemingly change, but the message never did. The Artist brooded over His masterpiece so intently because He saw the changes it would go through before it reached its destination. It began as an extraordinarily bright and glorious piece. He glowed with joy as it shined throughout the galaxy. As time passed the colors began to gray and fade. He began to grieve over His masterpiece, but He knew this would not be its permanent fate.

     Then the time came when He begin to set its restoration forth. The Artist with tender strokes of words began to create new strokes upon the canvas. These strokes would build upon one another only for a time to cover over the gray fading canvas. The Artist knew He was going to employ the most amazing shade of Color to repair this masterpiece. This Color was unlike any other color that had graced His palette. This Color held the costliest hue to have ever existed. It was held in reserve never to be tainted by the other paints upon the Artist's palette. Then at the very moment and fullness of time He spoke this Color into the earth. It saturated with the width and length and depth and height of the canvas. Soon this masterpiece found its full destiny in the gallery of Heaven.

It is this moment that I allow myself to open to You

A place in which I never thought I would find myself

Truly afraid because I do not want to have my heart broken

Being swept up by my love not knowing where it will take me

December 22, 2006

A Beautiful Picture

Every choice of color upon the brushes is a word carefully chosen

Every sweep of the brush over the canvas of my heart is a word of hope spoken

Every wondrous shade you create is a deeper affection for you

Every moment the picture being painted becomes ever clearer I am drawn so much closer

You paint a beautiful picture

Not Alone

There is a place and time

where u wonder why

u find urself so lonely

and ur not even alone

u laugh to urself saying, "why do i feel this"

when ur not alone

and ur amid the most amazing adventure

perhaps ur alone only becuz ur afraid

afraid to carry on

ur life spent every step so carefully made

now by impulse u live

living to the fullest measure

alone becuz u know u must embrace the fear inside

to conquer the loneliness

move to the forefront of this fight

eyes wide open arms ready to embrace

moving forward enveloped by this new life

then...it happens

the newness of life becomes the greatest friendship

this life begins to drive u

to push u foreword into the overabundance of life

lonely no more shall u feel for all the days of ur life

Dreamt a Dream

Dreamt a dream last night

Surely You were here

Love was at its height

In this dream I feared that of You I would lose sight

For in that moment I danced with You so near.

Fleeting Moments

Experiencing something that you've never felt before

Allow yourself to be overtaken by this

Never seeing the end of this dance

Swirling, Spinning, Swirling, Spinning

Waiting there is the Partner that we were all intended for

He says, "take my hand; for all will be yours."

Undeniable you take His Hand

Crash, Bang, Crash, Bang

All of what you were experiencing now comes to one choice

A choice you know you must make

You take His hand and forsake all else

Sweeping, Gliding, Sweeping, Gliding

He says My burden is light and My yoke easy

The pain and anguish lighten and is forgotten in time

You hang on to this hope believing that this Partner is right

Dancing, Swirling, Dancing, Swirling

To those with the heart of David

With all praise to the great and glorious Creator

Praise, Glory, and Honor unto You

The waves of the mighty ocean clap with praises unto you

The earth trembles and quakes and shouts Your glory

All creatures in heaven and earth give all honor due You

Praise, Glory, and Honor unto You the creator of the universe

My heart is torn between two worlds; two ideas

One is that of being good; the other says what the hell

I am enraptured by this other idea

God, I need you more now than ever

Being swallowed up can't grasp the edge

Where do I go from here---drowning, drowning

I will try to reach higher now

Taking hold of my Father's hand; pull me into Your bosom

Caress my hair with forgiving love

Validation

In love,

In sex,

In personhood,

In family,

In education,

In the way we speak,

In the way we act,

And carry ourselves,

Such an important part of ourselves, but

carries no weight unless you feel valid within yourself

Validation

The Creator

You wrote on the pages of eons

You envisioned your creation before time

You imagined all that you desired

You sacrificed the Lamb and time began

You spoke words; all was manifested

You breathed life; all was animated

This poem was written as a Christmas gift for Mr. F. Stacy and fellow teachers at E.C.C.S.

2006

Our Gifts We Bring

Our gifts we bring

Unto you our King

Never our own

Only to be shown

On this earth to You we glorify

First it is to self we die

It is to others we give

A life in You we live

Our gifts we bring

Unto you our King

To this earth you humbly came as a babe in a manger

Your Father gave you unto us Divinity with put upon flesh

A life planned out before the foundation of the earth

Your life quietly led until you took up the call

A beacon of light started as a flicker now a flame in the heart of man

A most perfect sacrifice so willingly given yet You live on

Daisy

In a field of daisies

My eyes focus upon You

A rarity among so many

Your splendor captivating

But we all, with unveiled face, beholding as in a mirror the glory of the Lord, are being transformed into the same image from glory to glory, just as by the Spirit of the Lord.

2 Corinthians 3:18

Moving from

stage to stage

glory to glory

A sense of wonder overtakes me

You overshadow my heart with life

You consume my spirit with fire

You who declared me to be Yours from the womb

Your love for me unbound by space and time

You swallowed my sin in pure blood

You made me to stand upright

You Have No Idea Because You Won't Let Go

Fear Not I Am With Thee...Enough Said

God You Are Awesome

I Began To Weep

With Tears Of Joy

God You Are Awesome

God You Are Awesome

You Pull Me Closer

Wanting Me Face To Face

God You Are Awesome

God You Are Awesome

Then My Heart Joins You

In This Symphony of Love

God You Are Awesome

God You Are Awesome

You Take Me Higher and Higher

You Take Me Into Deeper Depths

God You Are Awesome

God You Are Awesome

Direction

Quite a few years ago my daughter and I decided to go to Chattanooga, Tennessee. It was the first time I decided not to drive my usual route. In addition, I didn't prepare for the trip days in advance. The trip began uneventful and the directions I wrote seemed to be working well. That is until I reached Highway 41 with its many north and south exits. As I saw the many exits I began to question my ability to read and write my own directions. After debating with myself I began to believe that I was going the wrong way. I mistakenly took the north exit because I refused to accept that I could have written the wrong directions. This could have been easily corrected if I heeded the signs that clearly said I was going the wrong way. I travelled 35 miles before I decided to turn around and get back on the right path.

How often do we make decisions in life? How often do we forget to ask God what He thinks? Or How often do we intentionally leave God out of our decision processes? When we leave God out of the decision-making process it seems everything will go well. Then we find we've gotten lost somewhere along the road of life. In life there are many roads to choose, but we must remember the highways have been clearly marked. God clearly shows us which path to take in life in His word. It becomes our choice to take the right highway and pay attention to signs along the way. Even when we make a wrong turn God was gracious enough to provide a way to return to the right path. He made a way through His Son Jesus to return to Him. It is with utmost importance that we go to the Father first in our decision processes.

Nothing is ever too small for us to bring to Him. He yearns for us to seek His wisdom in everything we do.

Joshua 1::5b-9; Psalm 66:19-20; Proverbs 3:5-6; Philippians 4:6; Hebrews 13:5-6; James 1:5-6

when we meet on this lonely highway called life

there are many on ramps and exits

we get lost here—find our way there

when we come to the intersection called decision

do we stop and stay in the midst or pass on by

we all travel this road called life

we begin alone and somewhere on our journey

we find You and begin to walk hand and hand

A song based on Micah 4

Micah 4

Now it shall come to pass in the latter days that the mountains of the Lord's house shall be established on the top of the mountains and shall be exalted above the hills.

(This portion is spoken)

Every tribe, every tongue, every nation—Everyone

Worship (repeat 3x)

Come let us go to the mountain of the Lord

The House of the Lord of Jacob

Every tribe, every tongue, every nation—Everyone

Worship (repeat 3x)

He will teach us His way

We shall walk in His way

Every tribe, every tongue, every nation—Everyone

Worship (repeat 3x)

Dedicated to Rhonda P.

October 10

To the Head Cheerleader of God

Lost in the reverie of those words

"bumble bee tuna" that spilled from your lips.

I felt the room explode with His presence

when you lifted His name up.

The days I heard you cheer numbered a few,

but you penetrated my very soul.

Your light shined out across many, many fields, gymnasiums,

and churches it became a fiber of their (all of ours) very

existence.

You captivated the audience with the love you

enveloped us with.

In the end the audience so easily returned the love

you gave charitably.

To the Head Cheerleader of God

Amazing

I sit here amazed at Your presence everywhere

I hear Your voice in in the wind that whispers through the tall blades of grass

The winged creatures flutter by and I know You will carry me through the storms of life

As the heat of the sun kisses my skin I come to know and understand Your embrace and Your fire deep within me

I hear the song of heaven with every raindrop playing their chords upon the leaves

As the bees dance the dance of love I am in awe of the love You bestow upon me even in my darkest hours

I sit here and I drink in Your presence all around

You are amazing

Your river of life washes over me in Your light of

glory as I bow before You

Your river of life is overflowing the banks of my spirit

spilling out into the open space of this world

Your river of life feeds the life force that has made His

inhabitation within me

Your river of life heals the parched and death ridden land

and life is restored

Your river of life runs over with love for me and mankind

bringing peace to the chaos filled earth

11-July-2007

The further I stuffed my emotions the greater the cavern of emptiness I dug

A cavern like a dagger piercing to my innermost soul bringing the embrace of death

Like a fire death consumes without discriminating that which is dead and that which still holds life

The cry of my soul is deafening, but unheard by those surrounding me

The cry held in a stranglehold of my own refusal to let the dam of emotions to burst forth

For just one moment I loosen my grip; the dam begins to splinter then Your presence floods my inner being

An uncontainable force resurrecting and renewing murdered emotions birthing life once more.

Heartbroken

You pick up the shattered pieces of my heart to make me new again

For all that I am in life It all belongs to You

You never left me even when I chose to leave You

My heart no longer broken I give it all to You

Everything I say and do be it to glorify You

I hear Your whisper in the wind Your spirit speaking to mine

It's a melody of love so sweet of mysteries and wonders

Sweep me up in Your whispers in the wind

Obstacles

As I sat one night over a friend's home watching a cartoon with their son I found one of the closing scenes to be intriguing because the characters spoke a few profound, but simple words. Those words hold a truth for all of us.

In this scene several child sized ninjas were digging a rather large pit in the ground. They placed a carpet over the pit to hide it from their unsuspecting victim. Upon finishing the trap, they began to jump fervently on the carpet to test its collapsibility. As they jumped upon the carpet it did not collapse. Comically, they all looked questioning what was the problem. At the very moment the carpet gave way and they all fell into the pit. In the next scene, the ninjas lay in wait hiding from their victim. The victim's horse drawn chariot passed over the carpet covered pit and it didn't collapse. The ninja in the chariot then looks at them and says, "An obstacle is only and obstacle if it is perceived to be."

How many times in life do we approach situation with a defeatist attitude? Sometimes we treat situations as an automatic failure because we can't see the result. Perhaps we have been in a place in life before and we automatically assume our previous experience has dictated a negative outcome. Obstacles in life are only obstacles if you have determined they will become one. An adage says, "Don't make a mountain out of a molehill." These two are far different in comparison. Mountains require equipment and rigorous climbing to reach the summit. On the other hand, a molehill requires a simple step to overcome. Your ability to overcome an obstacle lies in your understanding the difference between the two. When you encounter a mountain that seems insurmountable we have been given a deliverer in Jesus to help change our perception. It is our choice to develop our faith in Him. Will we nurture it and use it, or will we squander it away? In Matthew 17: 20-21, Jesus deals with unbelief in ourselves. In this scripture there are three specific instructions to deal with unbelief. First, you must speak to the mountain. In many situations you must speak directly to the situation so that the enemy and most importantly you may hear that you will be victorious over the mountain. Next, prayer is a necessary and active means of communication between you and God. Active communication comes from our submission and willingness to sit and listen to God. If our lives are totally yielded unto Him we can be assured that God has an answer waiting for an open heart and spirit that is ready to receive. The last and final instruction that I find from personal experience that works is fasting. This is crucial because it requires a great sacrifice of self. Fasting requires you to shut yourself off from all fleshly desires. During the fast you should be reading the Bible and praying. These three combined: speaking, praying, and fasting will allow you to overcome the mountains in life. God is calling us into a place in which we never question whether we can make it over an obstacle, test, or situation.

In closing, if you come across a carpet in the road of life and are uncertain if there are deep pits of failure below do not look to the left or right for the enemy that lies in wait. Look unto Jesus He is waiting for you to call unto Him, pray, and fast knowing He will deliver you from the pit of the enemy.

About the Author

Greta E. Moon is the mother of four children: Alexis, 28, Kaitlin, 26, Kendall 22, and Josiah 8. She currently lives in Montgomery, Alabama. When she is not writing she enjoys spending time outdoors hiking and camping. She holds a degree in Biblical Studies from the International College of Bible Theology.

Greta has helped lead a teaching and worship conference for over 800 youth in Nakuru, Kenya. She has been to Acuna, Mexico to build a clinic and distribute food to the poor.

Greta has worked stateside on several mission projects building relationships with homeless populations to provide clothing, outdoor gear, food, and other essentials in Missouri, Arkansas, and Tennessee.